NATURAL PHENOMENA

HUMPBACK WHALE
MIGRATION

by Alexis Burling

FOCUS READERS

WWW.FOCUSREADERS.COM

Focus Readers is distributed by North Star Editions:
sales@northstareditions.com | 888-417-0195

Produced for Focus Readers by Red Line Editorial.

Content Consultant: Dr. Alexander J. Werth, Trinkle Professor of Biology, Hampden-Sydney College

Photographs ©: Ethan Daniels/Shutterstock Images, cover, 1; Velvetfish/iStockphoto, 4–5, 17; Intrepix/Shutterstock Images, 7 (background); Roman Art/Shutterstock Images, 7 (foreground); Iuliia Sheliepova/Shutterstock Images, 9; Lynn_Bystrom/iStockphoto, 10–11; wildestanimal/Shutterstock Images, 13; Nicola Destefano/Shutterstock Images, 14; Chase Dekker/Shutterstock Images, 18–19; John Tunney/Shutterstock Images, 20; Sean Lema/Shutterstock Images, 23; Lya_Cattel/iStockphoto, 24–25; Jewelsy/iStockphoto, 27; dikobraziy/Shutterstock Images, 29

ISBN
978-1-63517-908-8 (hardcover)
978-1-64185-010-0 (paperback)
978-1-64185-212-8 (ebook pdf)
978-1-64185-111-4 (hosted ebook)

Library of Congress Control Number: 2018934030

Printed in the United States of America
Mankato, MN
May, 2018

ABOUT THE AUTHOR

Alexis Burling has written dozens of articles and books for young readers on a variety of topics including current events, animals and nature, and biographies of famous people. She lives with her husband in the Pacific Northwest, where she loves to hike on the rugged coast and watch humpback whales migrate in the ocean below.

TABLE OF CONTENTS

CHAPTER 1

A LONG JOURNEY

Deep in the ocean, a humpback whale flaps its huge tail. Two other whales follow behind. The whales swim for many days. They travel from Alaska to Hawaii. Later that year, they will swim all the way back. In total, they will travel 6,000 miles (9,600 km) each year. This is one of the longest journeys made by any **mammal**.

Humpback whales are some of the largest animals in the world.

Unlike some whales, humpbacks live in both **hemispheres**. They can be found in all the world's oceans. Several groups of humpbacks live in each ocean. The whales in each group follow a different route when they migrate.

For example, some humpbacks live in the eastern and central part of the Pacific Ocean. These whales live in the Northern Hemisphere. They swim between Hawaii and Alaska. Other humpbacks live in the Southern Hemisphere. They travel to and from waters off the coast of Antarctica.

In the spring, humpbacks swim to their feeding grounds. The water there is cooler, and more food is available. In the fall, humpbacks change direction. They swim back to their breeding grounds, where the water is warmer. Humpbacks go there to breed and have babies.

Unless they are in trouble, humpbacks never migrate alone. They swim in groups.

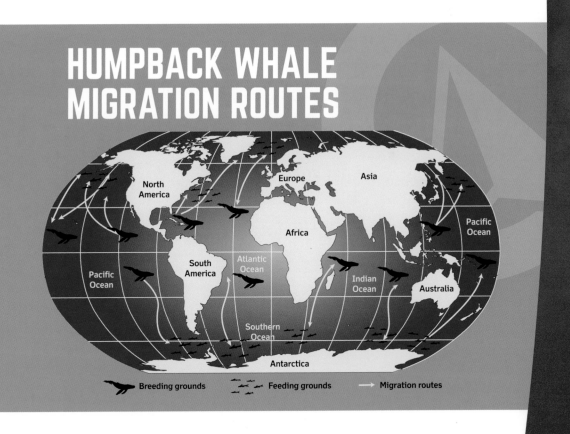

HUMPBACK WHALE MIGRATION ROUTES

North America

Europe

Asia

Pacific Ocean

Africa

Pacific Ocean

South America

Atlantic Ocean

Indian Ocean

Australia

Southern Ocean

Antarctica

Breeding grounds   Feeding grounds   Migration routes

A group of whales is called a pod. Most pods have two or three whales. There is a female whale and her **calf**. A male may swim with them to protect them. But sometimes the males race ahead to reach the feeding grounds sooner. Sometimes several pods travel together.

AN EPIC SHOW

Humpback whales can leap out of the water. This is called breaching. Their bodies go high into the air. Then they fall back with a big splash. No one knows why humpback whales breach. Some scientists think it helps brush sea creatures off the whales' backs. Or it may be a way to communicate. Other scientists say the whales are just being playful.

A humpback whale breaches in Kenai Fjords National Park in Alaska.

Humpbacks are slow but powerful swimmers. They move through the water at 3 to 9 miles per hour (5 to 15 km/h). Humpbacks can be 63 feet (19 m) long. Some weigh as much as 80,000 pounds (36,000 kg). But a humpback's huge size does not stop it from traveling great distances.

CHAPTER 2

WHY MIGRATE?

Humpback whales are always on the move. They migrate to find food. Like most other whales, humpbacks eat during only half of each year. In the summer, they swim toward the North Pole or the South Pole. Water in these areas is cooler. There, the humpbacks feed on **krill**, **plankton**, and small fish.

Humpback whales scoop water and fish into their large mouths.

A humpback whale can eat as much as 3,000 pounds (1,360 kg) of food each day. As a humpback eats, it builds up thick fat called blubber. This fat stores energy. Humpbacks can use this energy instead of food. They can go for several months without eating. By fall, they have built up enough blubber to survive the winter.

Then humpbacks migrate again. They swim back toward the **equator**. Here, they have their calves. Humpback calves are small. It is harder for them to stay warm in cold water. That is why humpbacks return to warm water to breed.

Before mating, male humpbacks compete for the attention of females.

A mother humpback swims near her calf.

They slap the water with their tails. This is known as lobtailing. Sometimes the whales do a kind of dance. They poke their heads above the water and glide. This is called spy-hopping.

A humpback slaps its tail on the water.

After two humpbacks mate, the female whale is pregnant for 11 months. Then she gives birth to a calf. A humpback calf weighs approximately 1,500 pounds (700 kg). It can be up to 16 feet (4.9 m) long. A calf stays close to its mother for approximately a year. The mother teaches it to swim and find food. Soon, the calf is ready to migrate. It swims with its mother back to the feeding grounds.

ONE OF A KIND

A humpback's long flippers and huge tail make it a strong swimmer. A humpback has the largest flippers of any whale. Its flippers can be one-third as long as its entire body. A humpback's tail has two sections called flukes. Together, the flukes can be up to 18 feet (5.5 m) wide. Every whale's flukes are unique, similar to a human's fingerprints. Each one has its own color and shape.

WHALE SONGS

Humpback whales can make a wide variety of noises. Some noises sound like squeaks. Others sound like low growls. But humpbacks are most famous for their songs. A song is a pattern of sounds. It can include howls, moans, and screeches.

Only male humpbacks sing. The males in a group sing the same song. But this song gradually changes over time. A whale may add or change parts of the pattern. The other whales in the group copy these changes, too.

A humpback's song usually lasts 15 minutes. But sometimes humpbacks sing for more than an hour. The sound carries for thousands of miles. It can be heard all the way across an ocean.

Scientists are not sure why humpbacks sing. The songs may help the whales communicate.

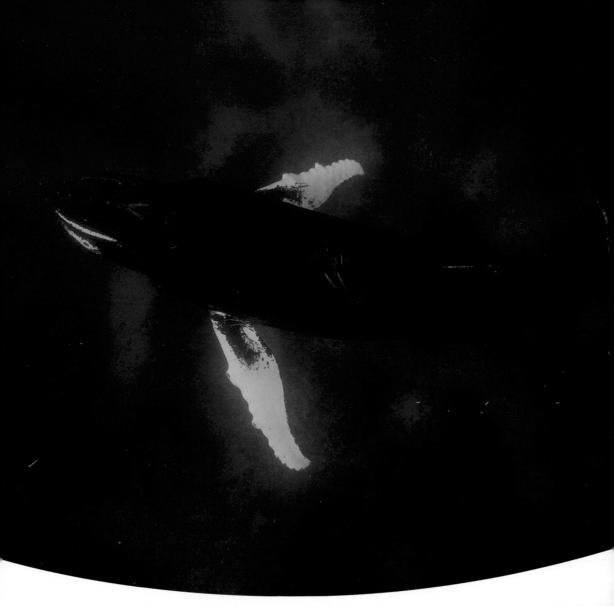

Humpbacks in the Atlantic Ocean make different sound patterns than humpbacks in the Pacific Ocean.

Or the males may hum to attract females. Another idea is that humpbacks sing to express happiness.

CHAPTER 3

HUNTING HUMPBACKS

Humpbacks do not have many natural **predators**. Their main dangers come from humans. For many years, whale hunting was common around the world. In Japan and Greenland, people hunted humpbacks for food. People in Alaska and Norway killed humpbacks to get blubber. They burned it to make oil for lamps.

Orcas are one of the few animals that pose a threat to humpbacks.

A humpback whale's baleen hangs down from its top jaw. It looks like stiff hairs.

Baleen was also popular in many countries. Humpbacks have baleen instead of teeth. This hard tissue forms inside a humpback's mouth. Whales use baleen to strain food such as fish and krill out of the water. People used baleen to make tools, toys, and piano keys.

From the 1600s to the early 1900s, people killed hundreds of thousands of humpbacks. Very few humpbacks were left. It looked as if these whales might become extinct.

HUMPBACKS VS. ORCAS

Orcas are fierce hunters. They have sharp teeth and can swim quickly. For this reason, they are sometimes called killer whales. Orcas are known to eat humpback calves. But sometimes humpbacks fight back. They may even defend other animals from orcas.

Then people took action. In 1966, the International Whaling Commission made **commercial** humpback whale hunting illegal. The United States passed the Endangered Species Conservation Act in 1970. This law aimed to protect plants and animals that were in danger of dying out. It included humpbacks. The law later became the Endangered Species Act in 1973.

The Marine Mammal Protection Act was passed in 1972. This law put stronger rules in place to keep humpbacks and other marine mammals safe. Capturing or killing humpback whales was no longer allowed. And products made from baleen

Several humpback whales gather to eat near Juneau, Alaska.

could not be sold in or brought to the United States.

With the help of these laws, the threat of hunting was gone. Humpback whales could migrate, mate, and have more calves. And the number of humpbacks began to grow.

CHAPTER 4

DANGERS ALONG THE WAY

Today, thousands of humpbacks swim in the world's oceans. But they still face many dangers. One threat is boat traffic. Hundreds of boats sail along the humpbacks' migratory routes. Some humpbacks get hit by large ships. Others are run over by whale-watching boats.

Whale-watching boats can harm migrating humpbacks.

In addition, many humpbacks get caught in fishing nets. Or they can get tangled in lines left in the water to catch lobster. Noise and **pollution** are bad for whales, too.

One of the biggest threats humpback whales face is climate change. As ocean

WHALE WATCHING

At least 13 million people go whale watching every year. Seeing these huge animals at home in the ocean is an exciting activity. But whale-watching boats sometimes hit humpbacks. The boats are noisy, too. Some humpbacks change their migratory patterns to avoid the traffic. This makes it harder for the whales to breed, rest, and find food.

Tourists watch whales swim in the Bay of Fundy off the coast of Nova Scotia, Canada.

temperatures rise, polar sea ice is melting. These changes affect where and when humpbacks can find food. If climate change continues, humpbacks may be forced to take different routes. Or they may have to migrate at different times.

Scientists carefully track how these problems are affecting humpbacks. They look for areas where humpback whales still need help.

In 2015, scientists put humpbacks into 14 groups. Each group lives in a specific part of the world. Four groups are endangered. One group is threatened. But nine groups are doing great. In fact, these nine groups were removed from the endangered species list in 2016.

Government protection is important for humpbacks. Other people can help these whales, too. Ship captains can learn to look out for humpbacks. Whale watchers can stay back on the shore. And people

can wait to throw fishing nets into the
ocean until whales are not in the area.

If people care for the oceans, the future
for humpbacks looks bright. These whales
can keep making their impressive journey
for many years to come.

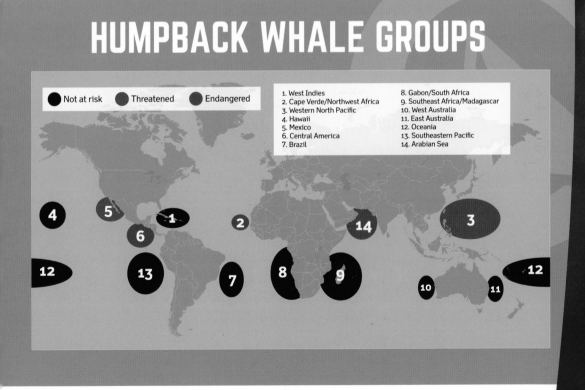

HUMPBACK WHALE GROUPS

● Not at risk ● Threatened ● Endangered

1. West Indies
2. Cape Verde/Northwest Africa
3. Western North Pacific
4. Hawaii
5. Mexico
6. Central America
7. Brazil
8. Gabon/South Africa
9. Southeast Africa/Madagascar
10. West Australia
11. East Australia
12. Oceania
13. Southeastern Pacific
14. Arabian Sea

FOCUS ON
HUMPBACK WHALE MIGRATION

Write your answers on a separate piece of paper.

1. Write a sentence summarizing the main point of Chapter 3.

2. Do you think whale watchers should be allowed to use boats? Why or why not?

3. Where do humpbacks swim in the spring?

   A. to their breeding grounds
   B. to their feeding grounds
   C. to the equator

4. What might cause a humpback to change its migration route?

   A. if the humpback has a calf
   B. if the humpback sees and hears many boats
   C. if the humpback swims in a group

Answer key on page 32.

GLOSSARY

calf
A baby or young humpback whale.

commercial
Done for the purpose of selling or doing business.

equator
An imaginary line that runs around the middle of Earth.

hemispheres
Halves of Earth. The Northern Hemisphere and the Southern Hemisphere are divided by the equator.

krill
Small animals that float in the sea and look similar to shrimp.

mammal
An animal that gives birth to live babies, has fur or hair, and produces milk.

plankton
Tiny creatures that often drift in big swarms in the ocean.

pollution
Harmful substances that collect in the air, water, or soil.

predators
Animals that hunt other animals for food.

TO LEARN MORE

BOOKS

O'Keefe, Emily. *Humpback Whale*. Minneapolis: Abdo
  Publishing, 2017.

O'Sullivan, Joanne. *Migration Nation: Animals on the
  Go from Coast to Coast*. Watertown, MA: Imagine!
  Publishing, 2015.

Read, Tracy C. *Exploring the World of Whales*. Richmond
  Hill, ON: Firefly Books, 2017.

NOTE TO EDUCATORS

Visit **www.focusreaders.com** to find lesson plans,
activities, links, and other resources related to this title.

INDEX

Answer Key: 1. Answers will vary; **2.** Answers will vary; **3.** B; **4.** B